Using N.L.P To Facilitate Spiritual Growth And Exploration

By Rex Morton

Using N.L.P To Facilitate Spiritual Growth And Exploration

Copyright Page

© 2023 by Rex Morton

All rights reserved. No part of this book may be reproduced in any form or by any electronic or mechanical means, including information storage and retrieval systems, without permission in writing from the publisher, except by a reviewer who may quote brief passages in a review.

This book is a work of non-fiction. Unless otherwise noted, the author and the publisher make no explicit guarantees as to the accuracy of the information contained in this book and will not be held responsible for any errors or omissions.

Published by Omniterra Media Inc

First Edition

Visit the author's website at www.rexmorton.com

For information regarding special discounts for bulk purchases, please contact Rex Morton @ Rex@rexmorton.com.

Disclaimer

This book is intended to provide information about the fields of Neuro-Linguistic Programming (NLP) and Cognitive Behavioural Therapy (CBT) and their potential integration. While the author has made every effort to ensure that the information was correct at the time of publication, the author does not assume and hereby disclaims any liability to any party for any loss, damage, or disruption caused by errors or omissions, whether such errors or omissions result from negligence, accident, or any other cause.

The contents of this book should not be used as a substitute for professional advice, diagnosis, or treatment. The reader should always consult with a qualified healthcare provider about any mental health concerns or conditions. Never disregard professional psychological or medical advice or delay in seeking it because of something you have read in this book.

The views expressed in this work are solely those of the author and do not necessarily reflect the views of the publisher, and the publisher hereby disclaims any responsibility for them.

The inclusion of websites, links, or references to other resources does not mean that the author or the publisher endorses the information the organization or website may provide or recommendations it might make. Furthermore, the author does not guarantee the accuracy of the information these resources provide.

The use of any information provided in this book is solely at your own risk.

A. Understanding the Essence of Neuro-Linguistic Programming (NLP)

Neuro-Linguistic Programming, commonly known as NLP, is a psychological approach that involves understanding the connections between neurological processes (neuro-), language (linguistic), and behavioral patterns learned through experience (programming). It suggests that these elements can be organized to achieve specific goals in life.

NLP was born in the 1970s, the brainchild of Richard Bandler, a mathematician, and John Grinder, a linguist. They were fascinated by the communication patterns and behavioral change mechanisms of exceptional therapists like Fritz Perls, Virginia Satir, and Milton Erickson. By observing these therapists, Bandler and Grinder believed they could replicate their effective techniques, creating a model for excellence that others could use.

Bandler and Grinder's approach relied on two fundamental concepts: the map is not the territory, and life and 'Mind' are systemic processes. The first implies that individuals create their realities based on their perceptions and experiences, not the objective world. According to the second, our bodies, societies, and the universe all interact with one another and have a mutually influencing effect on one another.

B. Connecting NLP and Spirituality: The Possible Synergy

At its core, spirituality concerns our search for meaning, for understanding our place in the universe, and for connecting with a higher consciousness or purpose. It often involves practices that help us to transcend our usual self-centered, ego-based consciousness and to experience a sense of unity with all of existence.

While NLP has traditionally been used for therapeutic purposes and personal development, its fundamental concepts and techniques are also highly relevant for spiritual growth. For instance, NLP can help us understand and change our internal 'maps' of reality, fostering a more profound, spiritual perception of the world.

The synergy between NLP and spirituality arises from their mutual focus on personal transformation. While spirituality provides the context and purpose for transformation, NLP provides practical tools and strategies to facilitate that transformation. By integrating NLP techniques into spiritual practices, individuals can potentially accelerate their spiritual development, achieving greater self-awareness, self-realization, and connection with their divine or universal nature.

C. Objectives of the Book

This book aims to provide a comprehensive guide to using NLP for spiritual growth and exploration. It is designed for anyone interested in spirituality, whether they are beginners on the spiritual path or long-time spiritual practitioners seeking new insights and tools.

The objectives of the book are as follows:

To introduce the principles and techniques of NLP and explain their relevance for spiritual growth.

To explore the synergies between NLP and various spiritual practices, including meditation, yoga, and energy healing.

To present practical strategies and techniques for using NLP in spiritual development, including self-reflection, visualization, anchoring, and timeline techniques.

To offer guidance on creating a personalized NLP-spirituality practice, including assessing spiritual needs and goals, choosing suitable NLP techniques, and evaluating progress.

To share real-life stories and case studies of individuals who have used NLP to facilitate their spiritual growth.

Through this exploration, the book hopes to empower readers to take control of their spiritual journey, using NLP as a tool to discover, explore, and transform their inner landscape, leading to a more profound, fulfilling, and enlightened existence.

A. History of NLP: Its Evolution and Key Contributors

Neuro-Linguistic Programming (NLP) emerged in the 1970s, initiated by Richard Bandler, a mathematician, and John Grinder, a linguist. Their joint fascination with the human mind and behavioral patterns led them to develop an innovative therapeutic approach that aimed to model human excellence and facilitate change.

Bandler and Grinder were particularly interested in the strategies employed by highly successful individuals, including esteemed therapists like Fritz Perls (Gestalt therapy), Virginia Satir (family systems therapy), and Milton Erickson (hypnotherapy). By analyzing and deconstructing their methods, Bandler and Grinder sought to create a framework that could replicate their effectiveness.

The resulting approach, dubbed Neuro-Linguistic Programming, combines insights from various fields including cognitive psychology, linguistics, and computer science. Since its inception, NLP has evolved, influenced by various contributors and adapting to new scientific discoveries.

B. Core Principles of NLP

NLP rests on several foundational principles:

The Map is Not the Territory: This principle highlights that our perception of reality (our map) is not objective reality (the territory). It's formed by our unique experiences, beliefs, and values, which filter our understanding of the world.

Life and 'Mind' are Systemic Processes: The systems that make up our existence (mind, body, society, and the universe) are interconnected and mutually influencing.

The Body and Mind are Parts of the Same System: This suggests that changes in our thought patterns can affect our physical state and vice versa.

If One Person Can Do Something, Anyone Can Learn to Do It: This principle is the bedrock of NLP's modeling technique. If a particular behavior or skill can be adequately modeled, it can be taught to others.

There is No Failure, Only Feedback: This principle promotes a growth mindset. If an approach doesn't work, it's not a failure, but feedback for adjusting the strategy.

C. Models and Techniques in NLP

NLP employs a variety of models and techniques designed to understand human behavior and facilitate change. Some key models and techniques include:

The Meta-Model: This language-based model is used to uncover deeper structures of a person's experience based on their speech.

The Milton Model: Contrary to the Meta-Model, the Milton Model uses vague and metaphorical language to stimulate the unconscious mind and facilitate change.

Anchoring: This technique involves creating an association between a particular stimulus and a specific emotional response.

Swish Pattern: A technique used to replace an unwanted behavior or response with a more desirable one.

Visual-Kinesthetic Disassociation (VKD): Often used for dealing with traumatic memories, this technique involves observing one's experiences from a dissociated, third-person perspective.

D. Applications and Effectiveness of NLP

NLP has a broad range of applications across personal and professional spheres. These include therapy (to address phobias, anxiety, depression), personal development (to enhance communication, leadership, motivation), and coaching (for performance improvement and goal-setting).

NLP's effectiveness can vary depending on the skill of the NLP practitioner and the openess of the individual. However, many people have reported significant benefits, including improved self-awareness, better communication, increased confidence, and the successful resolution of longstanding issues.

While NLP isn't a panacea and has faced criticism regarding its scientific validity, it remains a popular approach for those seeking to understand and alter their behavioral patterns. As you venture further into this book, you'll discover how these principles and techniques can be applied not only for mental and emotional improvement but also for spiritual growth and exploration.

Chapter III: Deep-Dive into Spiritual Growth and Exploration

A. Defining Spirituality: Various Perspectives

Spirituality is a broad and often subjective concept, with numerous interpretations across different cultures, religions, and philosophical systems. At its core, spirituality relates to matters of the spirit or soul, as distinguished from physical or material concerns. It often implies a search for meaning, purpose, and a higher reality.

For some, spirituality is closely tied to religious beliefs and practices, providing a sense of connection to a divine entity or entities. For others, spirituality is more personal and experiential, connected to self-discovery and personal growth, often beyond the bounds of traditional religious structures. Some interpret spirituality as a connection to others and the world around them, fostering a sense of unity and interdependence. Despite these varying perspectives, common themes in spirituality include seeking purpose, understanding one's self, experiencing transcendence, and fostering connections.

B. Elements of Spiritual Growth: Awareness, Connection, Transformation

Spiritual growth involves evolving in one's spiritual life, often encompassing three key elements: awareness, connection, and transformation.

Awareness: This involves cultivating a deep understanding of one's self and the nature of existence. It often includes practices like mindfulness and meditation, aimed at fostering self-reflection and consciousness of the present moment.

Connection: Spiritual growth often fosters a sense of connectedness – to others, to nature, to the universe, or to a higher power or purpose. This connection can lead to feelings of compassion, love, and unity, breaking down boundaries of self-centered thinking.

Transformation: This is a shift in one's mindset, behaviors, and perceptions, often leading to a sense of enlightenment or awakening. Transformation may involve releasing old patterns and embracing new ways of being, often guided by spiritual principles or insights.

C. Spiritual Exploration: Methods and Approaches

Spiritual exploration is the active seeking and experiencing of spiritual growth. This can involve various methods and approaches, including:

Meditation and Mindfulness: These practices cultivate awareness, presence, and inner peace, often leading to deeper spiritual insights.

Prayer and Ritual: These can foster a sense of connection to a higher power, often providing comfort, guidance, and a sense of purpose.

Reading and Study: Sacred texts, philosophical works, and contemporary writings can offer spiritual wisdom and guidance.

Nature and Art: Connection with nature or engagement with art can foster a sense of transcendence, beauty, and interconnectedness.

Community and Service: Participating in a spiritual community or engaging in selfless service can foster feelings of unity, compassion, and purpose.

D. The Role of Spirituality in Human Life

Spirituality plays a significant role in many individuals' lives, offering a sense of meaning, purpose, and belonging. It can provide a moral or ethical framework, guiding actions and decisions. Spirituality can also offer comfort and hope during difficult times, helping individuals cope with challenges and loss.

Furthermore, research has linked spirituality to various mental and physical health benefits, including lower levels of stress and anxiety, better coping with illness, and increased longevity. Spirituality can also foster a sense of gratitude, joy, and inner peace, contributing to overall well-being and quality of life.

In the next chapters, we will explore how the principles and techniques of NLP can support and accelerate spiritual growth, providing practical tools for fostering awareness, cultivating connection, and facilitating transformation.

Chapter IV: Intersection of NLP and Spirituality

A. The Neurological Basis of Spiritual Experiences

Recent advances in neuroscience have shed light on the neurological basis of spiritual experiences. Neurotheology, or spiritual neuroscience, is an emerging field studying the relationship between the brain and spirituality. Researchers in this field use neuroimaging technologies to examine brain activity during spiritual practices such as meditation and prayer.

Such studies have shown that specific areas of the brain are associated with spiritual experiences. For example, changes in the parietal lobe activity have been linked to experiences of self-transcendence and unity. Increased activity in the prefrontal cortex has been associated with focused attention during meditation. The limbic system, which regulates emotions, also plays a critical role in spiritual experiences, which often involve profound emotional responses.

Understanding the neurological basis of spiritual experiences can inform the use of NLP in spiritual growth. By using techniques that stimulate specific brain areas or replicate the neurological patterns of spiritual experiences, NLP may potentially facilitate similar experiences, enhancing spiritual awareness and fostering a sense of connection.

B. NLP as a Tool for Spiritual Exploration: A Conceptual Framework

NLP provides a practical framework for exploring spirituality. Here's how it aligns with key elements of spiritual growth:

Awareness: NLP techniques like mindfulness and perceptual positions can foster self-awareness and presence, fundamental aspects of spiritual exploration. By helping individuals understand and reshape their internal 'maps,' NLP can also facilitate a more profound, spiritual perception of reality.

Connection: NLP techniques such as anchoring and association can be used to foster a sense of connection, for example, by linking specific stimuli to states of unity or compassion. The use of metaphor, a powerful tool in NLP, can also facilitate spiritual understanding and connection.

Transformation: NLP is fundamentally about change. Techniques such as reframing, parts integration, and belief change can support spiritual transformation, helping individuals shift away from limiting patterns and embrace more empowering, spiritually-aligned ways of being.

C. Case Studies: Examples of Spiritual Growth Facilitated by NLP

Case Study 1: Mary, a yoga teacher, was struggling with a persistent feeling of disconnection from her spiritual practice. Through a series of NLP sessions, she worked on reshaping her internal representations of her practice, using visualization and anchoring techniques. These shifts enabled her to reconnect with her practice, experiencing a renewed sense of unity and spiritual fulfillment.

Case Study 2: John, a businessman, was seeking more purpose in his life. An NLP practitioner helped him explore his values and beliefs, using the values elicitation and belief change techniques. This exploration led to a profound shift in John's understanding of his purpose, facilitating a spiritual awakening that transformed his perspective on life and work.

Case Study 3: Emma, a therapist, was experiencing spiritual burnout, feeling cut off from her spiritual source. She embarked on an NLP-based spiritual exploration, using techniques such as perceptual positions and timeline therapy. These techniques helped her gain new spiritual insights and reignite her spiritual connection, leading to increased well-being and professional satisfaction.

These case studies illustrate the potential of NLP as a tool for spiritual exploration. In the subsequent chapters, we will delve deeper into specific NLP techniques and how they can be applied to foster spiritual growth.

Chapter V: NLP Techniques for Spiritual Development

A. Self-Reflection and Self-Dialogue through NLP

NLP provides techniques for effective self-reflection and self-dialogue, essential elements for spiritual development. The NLP Meta-Model, for instance, encourages in-depth self-inquiry, using questions to explore and challenge personal assumptions, beliefs, and values.

Through self-dialogue techniques, NLP helps in integrating different aspects of the self (referred to as 'parts' in NLP), fostering wholeness and internal harmony. Techniques such as the Visual Squash or Parts Integration allow for conversations between different parts, leading to resolution of internal conflicts and enhanced self-understanding.

B. Visualization Techniques for Spiritual Exploration

Visualization is a powerful tool in both NLP and spiritual practice. In NLP, visualization techniques often involve creating a mental 'movie' to rehearse desired behaviors or generate resourceful states. For spiritual exploration, visualization can be used to imagine spiritual concepts or experiences, such as a sense of unity with all beings, or a deep sense of peace and compassion.

The Swish Pattern is one NLP visualization technique that could be adapted for spiritual development. For example, you might visualize a current state of spiritual disconnection, and then 'swish' this image with a vivid image of feeling spiritually connected and fulfilled.

C. Utilizing Anchoring for Spiritual Grounding

Anchoring, an NLP technique based on classical conditioning, involves associating a specific stimulus with a particular state or response. This technique can be used for spiritual grounding - associating a specific sensory cue (e.g., a word, gesture, or object) with a state of spiritual connection or awareness. Once established, this anchor can then be used to quickly access the desired state, supporting regular spiritual practice.

D. Submodalities Work for Deep Spiritual Insights

Submodalities in NLP are the finer details of our internal representations, including visual (e.g., color, size, distance), auditory (e.g., volume, tone), and kinesthetic (e.g., temperature, texture) qualities. By manipulating these submodalities, we can change how we perceive and respond to our experiences.

For spiritual development, submodalities work can be used to amplify spiritual experiences or insights. For example, making a mental image of a spiritual experience larger, brighter, or closer can increase its emotional impact, deepening the spiritual insight.

E. Time Line Techniques for Spiritual Healing and Growth

Time Line Techniques involve working with our internal representations of time to resolve past issues and create a more empowering future. These techniques can be very potent for spiritual healing and growth.

For instance, past negative experiences or traumas that may be hindering current spiritual progress can be revisited and reinterpreted using the Visual-Kinesthetic Disassociation technique, promoting healing and release. Future pacing, another Time Line technique, can be used to imagine and 'pre-experience' desired spiritual states or achievements, fostering spiritual growth and alignment.

In summary, NLP offers a wealth of techniques that can be applied for spiritual development. While this chapter provides an overview, the subsequent chapters will provide detailed guides for using each of these techniques in your spiritual journey.

A. NLP and Meditation: Enhancing Mindfulness

Meditation and mindfulness are traditional spiritual practices that have gained widespread recognition for their benefits to mental and emotional health. NLP techniques can enhance these practices, making them more effective and personalized.

For example, the NLP technique of anchoring can be used to induce a meditative state more quickly and reliably. Anchors can be established during a deep state of meditation and then used to re-access this state when needed.

Additionally, NLP's emphasis on sensory awareness can enhance mindfulness practice. Techniques such as submodalities work can enrich sensory experiences and foster a deeper, more immersive state of mindfulness.

B. NLP and Yoga: Aligning Body and Mind

Yoga, a practice that involves body postures, breath control, and meditation, promotes physical health, mental clarity, and spiritual growth. NLP can complement yoga by fostering a strong mind-body connection.

NLP's visualization techniques can be particularly effective here. Visualizing the flow of energy through the body during yoga, or mentally rehearsing challenging postures, can enhance the yoga practice. NLP's belief change techniques can also help overcome mental barriers that may be hindering progress in yoga, such as self-doubt or fear.

C. NLP and Reiki: Balancing Energy for Growth

Reiki, a spiritual healing practice, involves the transfer of energy to promote healing and balance. It is based on the concept that an unseen life force energy flows through us, and that imbalance in this energy can lead to illness or stress.

NLP can support Reiki practice in various ways. For instance, NLP's visualization techniques can enhance the practitioner's focus during energy transfer. NLP techniques can also be used to prepare the recipient for the session, establishing a receptive, relaxed state.

D. NLP and Shamanic Practices: Exploring Ancestral Connections

Shamanic practices, which originate from indigenous cultures worldwide, involve connecting with nature and ancestral spirits for healing and guidance. These practices often use altered states of consciousness, achieved through techniques such as drumming, dancing, or plant medicines.

NLP's state management techniques can be useful in shamanic practices. For example, anchoring can be used to access specific states required for the practice. Techniques such as the Visual-Kinesthetic Disassociation can also provide a safe framework for exploring past traumas or issues, often a focus in shamanic healing.

Additionally, NLP's emphasis on symbolic thinking resonates with the symbolic nature of shamanic practices. Techniques such as metaphor use or dream interpretation can facilitate understanding of the messages or insights gained during shamanic journeys.

In summary, NLP can be a valuable addition to various spiritual practices, providing tools to enhance these practices and integrate their benefits more deeply into daily life. The subsequent chapters will provide more specific guides and examples of combining NLP with these practices.

Chapter VII: Potential Challenges and Ethical Considerations

A. Possible Limitations and Misinterpretations of NLP in Spiritual Practice

While NLP can be a powerful tool for spiritual growth, it's not without potential limitations and risks of misinterpretation. For instance, NLP models are simplifications of reality, not reality itself. If taken literally or used dogmatically, they can limit rather than expand one's perception.

Furthermore, NLP techniques involve manipulating one's internal experiences, which can be misused to avoid or suppress uncomfortable emotions or experiences. Spiritual growth often involves confronting and integrating such discomfort, not avoiding it.

Another potential limitation is that NLP focuses largely on the individual's subjective experience. It may not address social, cultural, or ecological dimensions of spirituality, which are central to many spiritual traditions and critical for a holistic approach to spirituality.

B. Ensuring Ethical Use of NLP for Spiritual Growth

Given the personal and sensitive nature of spiritual exploration, it's critical to ensure the ethical use of NLP in this context. Here are some guidelines:

Informed Consent: Individuals should understand what NLP involves and freely consent to its use. Any potential risks or discomforts should be clearly explained.

Respect for Autonomy: NLP practitioners should respect individuals' spiritual beliefs and values, and not impose their own. The goal of NLP is to facilitate individuals' own spiritual journey, not to shape it in a predetermined way.

Beneficence and Non-Maleficence: NLP techniques should be used with the intention of benefiting the individual and avoiding harm. This includes being aware of potential risks or negative effects and taking steps to mitigate them.

Confidentiality: Any personal or spiritual experiences shared in the context of NLP should be kept confidential, respecting individuals' privacy and dignity.

C. Coping Strategies for When Spiritual Exploration Gets Challenging

Spiritual exploration can sometimes bring up challenging emotions or experiences. This is a normal part of the process, as growth often involves facing and integrating unresolved issues. Here are some strategies for coping with these challenges:

Self-care: Ensure you are taking care of your physical, emotional, and mental health. This could include regular exercise, healthy eating, adequate rest, and time for relaxation and leisure.

Seek support: If you're finding the process challenging, don't hesitate to seek support. This could be from a trusted friend, a spiritual mentor, or a professional therapist.

Grounding Techniques: If you feel overwhelmed, grounding techniques can help. This could include mindfulness of your breath or physical surroundings, physical movement, or using NLP anchors associated with a calm, grounded state.

Remember the bigger picture: Spiritual growth can be challenging, but it's also a journey of self-discovery and transformation. Remembering the reasons why you embarked on this journey can provide motivation and perspective during challenging times.

In the subsequent chapters, we will delve deeper into these topics, providing a comprehensive guide for navigating the potential challenges and ethical considerations of using NLP for spiritual growth.

Chapter VIII: Creating Your Personalized NLP-Spirituality Practice

A. Assessing Your Spiritual Needs and Goals

Before embarking on a path of spiritual exploration using NLP, it's essential to assess your spiritual needs and define your goals. This assessment will be deeply personal, as spirituality is subjective and can mean different things to different people.

Consider questions like: What does spirituality mean to you? What are you hoping to gain or achieve through your spiritual journey? Are you seeking inner peace, a sense of purpose, or a deeper understanding of yourself and the world? Are you trying to overcome specific challenges or traumas? Your answers will provide a roadmap for your NLP-spirituality practice.

B. Choosing the Right NLP Techniques for Your Journey

Once you've clarified your spiritual needs and goals, you can select NLP techniques that align with these. If your goal is to achieve a greater sense of peace, for instance, techniques such as anchoring or visualization could be useful for accessing this state. If you're seeking to confront and overcome past traumas, Time Line Techniques might be appropriate.

Remember, there's no 'one-size-fits-all' approach here. The effectiveness of NLP techniques can vary greatly between individuals. It's important to remain flexible and open to trying different techniques, and see what works best for you.

C. Creating a Routine for Your NLP-Spirituality Practice

Consistency is key in any form of personal development, including spiritual growth. Therefore, it's crucial to establish a routine for your NLP-spirituality practice.

Consider factors like: How much time can you dedicate to your practice each day or week? What time of day do you feel most alert and receptive? What kind of environment supports your practice - quiet and secluded, or somewhere with the hum of life around you?

Also, consider integrating NLP techniques into existing spiritual practices. If you already meditate, for instance, you could include an NLP anchoring technique at the start or end of your meditation.

D. Evaluating Your Progress and Making Adjustments

Finally, it's essential to regularly evaluate your progress and make adjustments as needed. This isn't about judging your spiritual 'performance' but about staying attuned to your evolving needs and experiences.

Questions to consider could include: Are the NLP techniques you're using still serving your goals? Are there new challenges or goals emerging that require different techniques? Is your routine supporting your practice, or does it need tweaking?

Keep in mind, the journey of spiritual growth is a journey of discovery and learning, not a linear path towards a fixed destination. Be patient with yourself, celebrate your progress, and embrace the journey with an open heart and mind. The subsequent chapters will provide detailed guides and resources to support you in creating your personalized NLP-spirituality practice.

Chapter IX: Conclusion

A. Recapitulation of the NLP and Spirituality Synergy

The journey we have taken together in this book has explored the profound intersection of Neuro-Linguistic Programming and spirituality. We have delved into the fundamental principles of NLP, understanding its models, techniques, and potential applications. We've also explored the vast realm of spirituality, from defining what it means to different people to understanding the key elements of spiritual growth and the various approaches to spiritual exploration.

We have seen that NLP, with its focus on understanding and changing our internal mental processes, can be a powerful tool for spiritual growth. By providing techniques to alter our state of consciousness, challenge our limiting beliefs, visualize our spiritual goals, and anchor positive spiritual experiences, NLP offers a practical and effective approach to facilitating spiritual exploration and transformation.

B. Looking into the Future: NLP and Spirituality Research

As we look to the future, the synergy between NLP and spirituality holds great promise. Further research in this area can deepen our understanding of how these two fields can best support each other.

Research might explore, for example, the neurological basis of spiritual experiences, seeking to uncover how NLP techniques can stimulate or facilitate these experiences. Studies could also evaluate the effectiveness of specific NLP techniques for spiritual growth, providing evidence-based guidance for individuals embarking on their spiritual journey.

Moreover, there's vast potential for cross-pollination between NLP and various spiritual traditions, exploring how NLP can enrich practices such as meditation, yoga, Reiki, or shamanic journeys, as we have started to discuss in this book.

C. Final Thoughts and Encouragements

In conclusion, the integration of NLP and spirituality offers a unique and potent pathway for spiritual growth. However, it's important to remember that spirituality is a deeply personal journey, and there's no 'right' way to embark on this path. The aim of this book, and the NLP-spirituality practice we have proposed, is not to prescribe a fixed route, but to provide a toolkit that can be customized to your individual needs and goals.

As you embark or continue on your spiritual journey, remember that it's about progress, not perfection. There will be challenges and setbacks, but these are part of the process and opportunities for growth. Be gentle with yourself, stay open to learning, and celebrate your victories, no matter how small they might seem.

Finally, we encourage you to approach your NLP-spirituality practice with curiosity and joy. After all, the journey is as important, if not more so, than the destination. Embrace the adventure of self-discovery and transformation, and remember that you are not alone on this path. We hope that this book will serve as a supportive guide on your journey, and we look forward to hearing about your experiences and insights.

Rex Morton is a renowned author and researcher in the United Kingdom with a passionate interest in the human mind, specifically in Cognitive Behavioural Therapy (CBT) and Neuro-Linguistic Programming (NLP).

Morton has spent a considerable portion of his professional life diving deep into the theories and principles that form the backbone of these two compelling fields. His fascination with NLP led him to complete an extensive certification program, solidifying his understanding of this innovative approach to understanding human behaviour.

Although Morton does not have clinical experience, his intense curiosity and dedication to studying these subjects have made him a respected figure in the field. He has thoroughly researched the integration of NLP techniques into CBT, offering fresh perspectives and insights into how these two methodologies can complement each other to enhance understanding of human cognition and behaviour.

As an author, Morton has successfully communicated his knowledge and passion to a broader audience, making complex psychological theories accessible to professionals and interested laypersons. His writing is characterized by a clear, engaging style and a focus on the practical application of theories, making them relevant to everyday life.

In his personal life, Morton is an ardent lover of the natural world, often spending his free time exploring the British countryside. His passion for landscape photography allows him to capture and share the beauty of these excursions. Despite his accomplishments, Morton is known for his humility and eagerness to continue learning. His work continues to inspire those interested in the intricate workings of the human mind and the exciting possibilities presented by the integration of NLP and CBT.

If you've found the content of this book enlightening and wish to continue your journey of understanding the human mind, I warmly invite you to visit my website at www.rexmorton.com. The website serves as a hub of knowledge where I share my latest findings, thoughts, and insights on the integration of NLP and CBT.

I also encourage you to subscribe to the newsletter available on the website. By subscribing, you'll receive regular updates on a range of topics, from detailed discussions on specific NLP techniques and their application in CBT, to the latest research in the field.

The newsletter is also the first place I'll share news of upcoming releases. Whether it's the announcement of a new book, the launch of an online course, newsletter subscribers will be the first to know. This is a great opportunity to continue learning directly from me, deepening your understanding of NLP and CBT, and enhancing your skills in applying these techniques in your own life or professional practice.

I'm looking forward to sharing this journey with you.